HAL•LEONARD

INSTRUMENTAL
PLAY-ALONG

AUDIO
ACCESS
INCLUDED

PLAYBACK+
…d • Pitch • Balance • Loop

VIOLIN

T0066297

POPULAR HITS

To access audio visit:
www.halleonard.com/mylibrary

Enter Code
7710-4676-0153-6443

ISBN 978-1-61774-003-9

HAL•LEONARD®
CORPORATION
7777 W. BLUEMOUND RD. P.O. BOX 13819 MILWAUKEE, WI 53213

Visit Hal Leonard Online at
www.halleonard.com

BREAKEVEN

VIOLIN

Words and Music by STEPHEN KIPNER, ANDREW FRAMPTON,
DANIEL O'DONOGHUE and MARK SHEEHAN

THE CLIMB

from HANNAH MONTANA: THE MOVIE

VIOLIN

Words and Music by
JESSI ALEXANDER and JON MABE

FALLIN' FOR YOU

VIOLIN

Words and Music by
COLBIE CAILLAT and RICK NOWELS

Moderate Rock

To Coda $\oplus$

D.S. al Coda

CODA $\oplus$

FIREFLIES

VIOLIN

Words and Music by
ADAM YOUNG

HALO

Violin

Words and Music by BEYONCÉ KNOWLES,
RYAN TEDDER and EVAN BOGART

HEY, SOUL SISTER

Violin

Words and Music by PAT MONAHAN,
ESPEN LIND and AMUND BJORKLAND

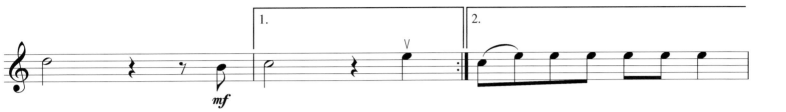

I GOTTA FEELING

Violin

Words and Music by WILL ADAMS,
ALLAN PINEDA, JAIME GOMEZ, STACY FERGUSON,
DAVID GUETTA and FREDERIC RIESTERER

I'M YOURS

VIOLIN

Words and Music by
JASON MRAZ

LOVE STORY

VIOLIN

Words and Music by
TAYLOR SWIFT

NEED YOU NOW

Violin

Words and Music by HILLARY SCOTT,
CHARLES KELLEY, DAVE HAYWOOD and JOSH KEAR

POKER FACE

VIOLIN

Words and Music by
STEFANI GERMANOTTA and REDONE

SMILE

Violin

Words and Music by BLAIR DALY, JEREMY BOSE,
MATTHEW SHAFER and JOHN HARDING

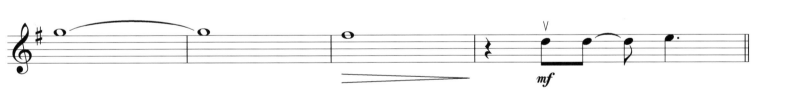

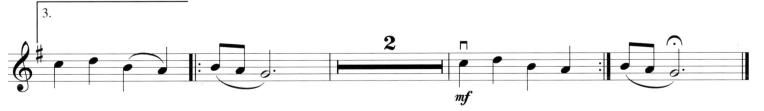

VIVA LA VIDA

VIOLIN

Words and Music by GUY BERRYMAN,
JON BUCKLAND, WILL CHAMPION and CHRIS MARTIN

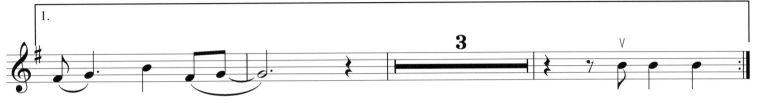

YOU BELONG WITH ME

VIOLIN

Words and Music by
TAYLOR SWIFT and LIZ ROSE

USE SOMEBODY

VIOLIN

Words and Music by CALEB FOLLOWILL, NATHAN FOLLOWILL
JARED FOLLOWILL and MATTHEW FOLLOWILL